THE BUSINESS OF ART

by

Antonio Moore

Introduction

Art, comes in many forms, styles and sold in many different price ranges. Every artist wants to be the next Warhol or Picasso but very few know the business side of how to market and sell art, let alone become a millionaire doing it. Whether you draw, paint, do graphics or any other form of art there is a market for it. It is up to you to find that market and how you can get your art to the buyers in the market of art you are in. Today with social media, apps and all the outlets available, you can share your art with the world with click of a button. This is something all artists should take advantage of. Build your brand at all cost and don't forget to know your worth! This is where research comes in but also its on you to determine what your worth is. Know your product, know your consumer and know your competition and what their work sells for. You should also know your location, the closest city with more art shows and happenings if yours isn't one of them. Know the restaurants who hang art on commission, educate yourself on the times of the year to market your art around holidays, all this will help point you and your art business in the right direction to be profitable and provide your service to a wide variety of customers. After you have done a few of these things it is time to keep the customers you have and have to goal be for your customers to be your walking advertisement to bring more customers.

The Drive

In any business, the number one thing any individual must have is Drive. This statement may be even more true in the Art World versus many other industries. Sure, you can get a degree in art, learn processes, Art History, Graphic Design and do many things to learn about art and how to apply art and the different periods of art, but who can tell you how to run a legitimate art business without working for someone? We all want to sell that Million Dollar piece or even a piece for one hundred thousand would satisfy most artists I know, but how do you keep the process going? Where do you sell? How do you find shows? How do you contact galleries who contact clients to know about your art? These are all questions I am sure a lot of artists such as myself have and it's a process like any other business.

My advice is first to find your niche! Find out what your strength is and push that over all other forms of art. Jumping around to various forms of art and not being as good in all forms may affect your brand and confuse buyers to who you really are. If you are an airbrush artist, trying to tattoo may be a challenge for you and put you up against guys who strictly tattoo. Same for a tattoo artist who feels they can paint on canvas and sell with no problem. Some can do both but some may not have an eye for what people like on canvas but have an eye for things people want tattooed, so marketing and knowing your market in each form of art is a big piece of information as well. I started out doing airbrush, moved to fabric paint on clothes and in 2008 I painted my first canvas. Canvas paintings has since been my main form of art and I am still learning new processes and new ways to paint on canvas almost a decade later.

Use your resources! Social Media is your best friend. Search shows in your area, become friends with other artists and see what shows they are attending and how they are selling their work. Eventbrite is another good tool to find art events in your area which normally has vending opportunities for art companies and other businesses. Art shows are another way to market yourself to clients looking to buy artwork. There are many shows that travel state to state and require you to register and be a part of the show. RAW Artists, Pancakes and Booze, Exposure Global Art shows and a few others are some that I have participated in personally and know they have a huge global following.

Drive in art will require a lot of time and dedication, it will also require travel, spending money on shows to display and much more. Remember to use your resources, find your niche and don't be scared to use other artists as resources.

WHAT FORM OF ART?

As mentioned briefly in the previous section, one of the most important things to know is what form of art you will be most known for. There are some artists with many strengths which is always a great thing but for branding and marketing purposes it would be smart to get your name well known for one form first, then branch out and show people other forms of art you offer. As I said I transitioned from Airbrush to fabric paint before touching a canvas. My main focus is only canvas paintings and paint parties. These are actually two different forms of art but once again I established myself as a painter on canvas before becoming a teacher and an event host with paint parties for various events. When you approach a person and tell them you draw, paint, airbrush, and do anime. Most people want to know which one you are best at. When a person does multiple things well, most would like to zero in on which they do best and that would most likely be the thing that most people pay for. That may simply because the thing you do most is simply the thing you are most professional at and why people are more likely to pay for that one particular area of your artwork. Once you figure out what form of art you are going to focus on then you want to find the market for that form of art. Every art like every product has its own target market with different age groups, income classes and more. We will discuss marketing and target markets for each group more in detail in the later chapters.

BUILDING RELATIONSHIPS

In any business and in life in general one of the most important things to do is build solid relationships. In the Art Business this is very important to having any success with sales and growing your market. The key to building relationships is knowing who your market is. When I first started airbrushing shirts in 2003 my immediate market were my friends and local hustlers who I know had fast money to spend to look different and get things customized. Me and my partner used to spend hours all day airbrushing out of his girlfriends' apartment (probably without proper ventilation) and when we didn't have orders we would do things to cater to our market at that time. We used to do pictures of rappers like Biggie, Tupac, 50 Cent and more who were popular at the time and all-time greats. I used to airbrush current video game covers like

Grand Theft Auto, Madden and more that I knew people would love and was something different to put on a shirt. After getting inventory done we would go to the local basketball courts and places in Aberdeen and Edgewood where we knew people were and most were hustlers with fast money to spend. This led to some days making $500 a day easily selling a good 10 shirts or more. This led to more clients and bigger projects including an annual order from the Minnesota Vikings through E.J Henderson. E.J ordered custom airbrushed shirts every year for training camp for the entire defense with a new Vikings theme. I did this for about 6 years in a row until E. J Retired from the NFL. This was a key relationship that led to an annual bulk orders and many other orders and opportunities working with E.J Henderson and his foundation. Working with Airbrush from 2003-2005 we built other key relationships including being contracted to airbrush at company events on Aberdeen Proving Ground, doing bulk shirts for local sports teams and more. In 2005 while attending Morgan State University a new trend started up north and was spreading like crazy, Hand painted shirts with fabric paint. At first, I wasn't big on the idea do to how long it would take vs airbrushing but after trying it I fell in love and ended up doing it more than airbrush. It was cheaper, no compressor, noise, and it was more durable when washed, it did not fade like airbrushed shirts looked after being washed. Doing fabric paint led to new relationships and opportunities. While at Morgan State I was about of a program called the Morgan M.I.L.E Program. This program was run by a professor named Dr. Desousa. He did a lot of great things centered around male leadership and community involvement. I was able to get a contract to make shirts for the whole organization and commissioned to do a painting for him as well. At the time there was a booming clothing line out of Philly named Miskeen. Their clothing was all hand painted abstract designs and they actually had artists like myself in a warehouse hand painting thousands of shirts and jeans per day. In 2006 I had an interview to work for them as an artist. For those who don't know the clothing line made $50 million in 2005 I believe. The office was in Camden, New Jersey which is south Jersey not far from Philadelphia. I went to the interview of course loaded with artwork on clothing. My work was more detailed in fabric paint than anyone else who was doing it at the time. I could actually do a portrait while others mainly did abstract. So, in the interview, the CEO of the company loves my work and wants me to join the team. The pay was one dollar per shirt and fifty cents each pair of jeans you produce. Of course to anyone that sounds like no money, but he said he had artists making one thousand dollars per week producing one hundred shirts and fifty jeans per day easily. The shirts retailed at fifty to eighty dollars and stores and the jeans even more. Even though it was a good opportunity to learn, grow and build more relationships I declined the chance. The fact was I was 22 years old at the time and no real means to just pick up and move from Maryland to New Jersey like it was nothing. I stayed in Maryland and continued to work as usual, I was just getting out of Morgan so I was finding what I wanted to do other than art to keep the bills paid. This time Myspace came out and the internet and social media actually were born to help all entrepreneurs and people connect around the world. Myspace led to more fans of more art, more people locally who could discover who I was before actually being present where I was and a lot more relationships. This is around the time I met the mother of my child as well so Life was changing in all directions along with the world changing for the better as far as technology goes. In 2008 while caring for an infant and working I was still mainly during fabric paint on clothes. I received an order from someone for something they can hang on their wall. My whole life I have only done clothes I had no idea even what to buy to paint on, I had no idea of what a canvas was at the time. Eventually I found a canvas and painted the portrait on canvas, with fabric paint. I had no idea what paint to use and I didn't even use a brush. The client hated it! No blending, all black and white with fabric paint, it was my first and I charged her seventy-five dollars. I believe I bought a 3 pack of canvas panels at the time, so I believe I had two more blank canvas left to do something else on. I eventually ended up painting Cal Ripken on one and a Ravens theme on the other. Facebook had begun its run around this time and it had become one of my best sources for spreading my work and gaining new clients. I posted them to Facebook and started to build new relationships with different people. One of my close friends who was a big ravens fan bout one of my canvas ravens themed and bought some stuff for his grandfather. His grandfather who owned a nice home and a nice Nissan 350Z became a regular customer of mine, wanting artwork for his bar and I even painted the 350Z logo on a car cover for him. Instantly after doing my first canvas my network of clients began to grow. I started to notice some love to hang stuff on their wall vs wearing art and people pay more for wall art vs wearable art. From there I started to do more canvas and the support was incredible. I did a few for E.J Henderson, my homeboy for the Vikings and a few other athletes I knew. Pretty soon orders were coming in for all sorts of canvas such as Ravens' and Orioles' artwork and pictures of peoples' kids. During this time, I had discovered another local athlete who was actually an artist himself had a foundation in Baltimore. We connected on Facebook and He contracted me to teach my t-shirt class to students at a local elementary school in east Baltimore. This was a big opportunity to build a relationship with an established person in the artworld and make a name for myself as an art teacher teaching my program I created teaching kids to hand paint shirts. The class was a big success, the kids loved it and it was a huge step in the direction of me having my own art school. Shortly after I reached out to an organization on Aberdeen Proving Ground named S.K.I.E.S Unlimited. This was an organization that held many programs with kids on the army base and kids of government contractors on the army base. Shortly after interviewing with them we developed a one-week t-shirt class program in which I taught kids to hand paint their own shirts using my whole process. The negotiation was eighty percent to me and twenty percent to their organization off each class but they handled all marketing, signups and even providing the location for the classes. This was a huge step in getting more contracts of this magnitude. We did about five classes with S.K.I.E.S with every class being a success. Kids were able to do very detailed shirts and I was able to make a good amount of money in a little amount of time to teach what I love. After doing canvas for a few years consistently I began to find art shows and even find my way to get my art to celebrities. One day I was coming from a concert in DC and come to my car to find a flyer for a Jeezy concert in Baltimore in the next 2 weeks. I end up seeing who the promoter was on the flyer and decide to try to message her about me getting Jeezy a painting. I dm her on Instagram and she replied telling me to call her Monday. I called her and explained what I do and what my plans were. She told me it's cool to do a painting for Jeezy and I can present it to him. I also told her about my wife having a nail salon and possibly being able to do her nails for shows and more. She loved the idea and I connected her and my wife on top of me getting the connection to get art to all the artists who she does concerts with. After that show I began doing shows for every rapper and singer who she brought to Baltimore which was about every two to three months. Through her also other promoters and entertainers started to look at me as the guy who does paintings for celebrities. The more celebrities I started to be in pictures with and do art for the more business I started to get from everyday people as well as other show promoters. One celebrity in particular I began to follow was former FUBU owner, Daymond John. I began to follow his business moves and pay attention to how he gave advice on entrepreneurs branding themselves. Following him led me to a place in New York called the Paley Center. This was a media center in Manhattan that held shows and events for Tv shows, Authors and more. I met Daymond here talking about his book "The power of Broke" I took the Megabus to new York and was actually at the event about an hour early. This led me to meet his staff and team who were there early to setup the event. They saw my painting and that I was first in line so they gave Daymond the Heads up early that someone had a painting for him outside. After being in the event and at conclusion, they had a Q AND A session. Of course, I stand up with my painting and ask how can I get him the piece. He does the best thing that could've happened which is bring my painting on stage for the crown to see. I get applause and he tells the crown he's going to give it to his mother. This was my first of many times at the Paley Center meeting many celebrities. I actually met Daymond here twice, the second time was when Shark Tank premiered and I met him along with Marc Cuban and Barbara Corcoran. In addition to them I was also able to meet Lee Daniels and the cast of the hit show STAR at the Paley Center as well. In 2014 a new trend had started in the art world, Paint Parties. These were parties catered to adults while they sip wine they are instructed to paint a particular picture. There was one big company who started initially and they were hiring artists like myself paying them eighty dollars per class and making hundreds and thousands. I decided I wanted to start doing my own parties versus working for another company. I looked on Youtube and other sources and looked into designs and more on how to start. I was vending with my shirts at a local bar and restaurant called Edgewood station and they had a nice eating area suitable to host a paint party. I was very cool with the owner and ran the idea by him. He loved it and thought it would of course bring him more business. I bought what I needed for the party which wasn't cheap getting things like easels for the first time but it was a success. I ended up having about nineteen people in total and everyone loved it. From there I ended up doing at least 10 more parties there over the next 6 months before they went under new management and I moved to another local restaurant in Edgewood named Venetian Palace. This was in a better location, they had a better and longer reputation and they had a private room I could use for parties. Most places charged a set fee to use party rooms but the advantage with Venetian Palace was they charged a minimum in food and drink to use the room. I offered one glass of wine per person so the big bottle of wine and whatever my guests ordered would cover the minimum with no problem. From These two places I began to do more parties in people's homes and more businesses started to open up to the paint party events. I formed a relationship with a local nursing home through a woman I knew off Facebook, and had done shirts and other art orders for. She coordinated events for Lorien Nursing Home in Belcamp. My first party was for the staff there for about twenty-five nurses and women in the medical field who worked and were contractors at Lorien. The class was a success and they immediately told me they would schedule more. The next class was for the elderly residents and their family members as a resident activity. The seniors did great and the family and nursing home loved the party and how therapeutic it was for the elderly. Along with classes, Lorien commissioned me to do a 60-foot mural in the building and other painting projects along with parties. This was a key relationship to getting contracts at their other locations as well. The paint parties sprung a lot of new business relationships that were beneficial to me and the person having the party. One of my biggest relationships was my partnership with my former college, Morgan State University. The coordinator for the student center wanted to host an event to raise money for a scholarship for the Young Alumni Association on campus. The first event we did in 2016 we had fifty-three people in attendance and raised over one thousand dollars for a scholarship. Of course I made one thousand dollars before my costs in a few hours as well. The second class we did in 2017 we had over 100 people attend, meaning we raised a two-thousand dollar scholarship and the company made close to two thousand before costs. Along with those two classes the contact for setting up those Morgan State classes transferred to Howard University and reached out to me to do the same deal at Howard. So, in doing paint parties I started to find that fundraising was the best marketing tool for the parties. Fundraising raises money for a good cause, the fundraiser gets to raise money and I get to make more lump sums having someone else sell tickets, market and provide the venue. In 2017 I began to vend at Initiative 71 compliant parties in Washington D.C. These parties were filled with people spending larger amounts of money buying Initiative 71 products. I did one or two and every one I did lead to me connecting and Building a relationship either with a new promoter or a club owner. In the process of about 8 months going to DC three times a week which was an hour from me I met bar and club owners from Adams Morgan to Connecticut Ave. which were the two most lucrative areas for clubs in DC. One of the bar owners is a guy by the name of Mike Romeo. I met him live painting at an event on the rooftop of one of his clubs. (notice I said one of his clubs) We chatted and once I realized he owned the place I donated an Audrey Hepburn piece I had to him to display in the club. He told me about an artist he helped blow up by painting in all his restaurants and clubs and that artist is now in Miami living good off art. We talked about how we could help one another and ideas we both had. In the process setting up shows, events, selling art in all his establishments in DC. This all came from setting up vending at a small event with about 40 people there.

In building relationships, you have to talk to people. You never know who's who and who can help change your life. I advise any artist to talk to any and everyone because you just never know! In building relationships, you also have to bring things to the table. It cant be all about benefitting you and not the other party. A good way to do this with art is to offer a percentage to people with wall space and traffic in exchange for displaying your art. Restaurants, barbershops, salons and anyone who has wall space and customers to buy it would be wise to build a relationship with and work out a deal that makes you both happy.

CONTRACTS

It doesn't matter how well you know someone, how long you have known them, make sure you get everything in writing when it comes to your art business. This goes for paint parties, art orders and anything related to exchanging money for your art services. When I was first starting out I had to learn the hard way and finding out that no contract causes a lot of confusion. I mentioned earlier teaching with the NFL player from Baltimore. The negotiation to teach with another organization he was connected to ran by Keion Carpenter called Shutdown Academy had a summer camp every year called C4C. I contacted them about doing my t-shirt program for their kids in July of 2011 I believe it was. I talked to the Reps and told them my fee and everything that was included. At the time I was charging twenty five dollars per student for shirt classes which was only about fifteen dollars profit after my supplies. I was going to charge their organization ten dollars per child because they said they had sixty kids. I knew I could get some things in bulk and maybe pay a little less in overhead. We agreed on me coming to teach but the week of the event I came down with the worst sinus infection I could ever imagine. I could not go to work, leave the house, take light, noise or anything. I ended up canceling the class because I was out sick for a week. Of course I was upset and felt I possibly blew an opportunity to work with a few well known locals and a great organization but I knew with social media emerging everyday it would not be my last chance at a big chance. A few months later I noticed the Player was having a week dedicated to his foundation. All week there were different events. I reached out to them but this time speaking to a different girl and told her I would like to teach and how I was supposed to teach in the summer but I got sick and the whole story. We agreed and I gave her a price over the phone and we discussed details of the class. The class was 35 students and took place at an elementary school in East Baltimore with mostly kids from low income families and in pretty rough neighborhoods. The day of the class it went good, I did a live painting and then let the kids do all their own individual shirts. The designs were traced in sharpie and it was the logo of the player. The kids were supplied with boards for the shirts, shirts, and about 3 bottles of fabric paint each totaling about 8 dollars per kid. After the class, I normally took my boards to put in between the shirts but on this day I allowed kids to keep the boards because the shirts were still wet. A few days later I reach out for my payment for the class, ten times thirty five students, three hundred and fifty dollars. The responses are definitely not what I expected. They treated me as if I wasn't supposed to request my money for my services. I guess the miscommunication between the different females from the summer camp to this camp changed and maybe she forgot our conversation about me telling her the price. I never once talked to the player only to set it up so of course he doesn't know my side of the story only his employees' side. Long story short after about 3 weeks of going back and forth I ended up getting a check and she messaged me with the attitude like She wasn't expecting to pay for me teaching 35 kids for two hours and spending on gas supplies and more. At the time I was on the brink of eviction from my apartment and more so waiting a few weeks to get money for work I did was a bad situation. I've seen both parties since then and we speak but I can tell the energy isn't the same after that incident. After that I began to have contracts for my paint classes on shirts and once I started my Sip and Paint parties I began to draw up contracts as well. When I first began I would charge a deposit to book and then take the deposit off of the total on the day of the event. This was good at first until I noticed I began losing with small parties. My minimum class is ten people and I had a few instances where people told me they had 17 booked and 8 show up to the class. This made my projections less and even led to me losing money on a few parties. All this confusion led to contracts and changed my deposit into a booking fee which does not come off of the total the day of the party. In the paint party contract I would state the minimum number of people, exactly what I provided, the amount of wine per person if any, every detail that can be thought of. I know two of my homeboys who are the area's best tattoo artists. They were posting tattoos of woman and people with tattoos in private areas. I helped them type up a contract for photo releases on social media to be able to post photos of people they tattooed for marketing purposes. No matter what you do, don't think it's too small for a contract. If it's a mural, make a contract for the deposit, who's paying for paint, time to finish and all you can think of so both parties know all details and what to expect from one another.

WATCH YOUR PEERS AND COMPETITION

Again, as it is with any industry, you have to watch your peers and competition. I have watched and learned from many artists through social media and from doing events and art shows networking with fellow artists. Other artists and your competition may be who you learn from the most. One local artist in Harford County I started to follow is a guy named Shawn Forton. He made his name doing sports art for Ravens football players and then spreading to other teams and other industries. I never knew him personally until social and we eventually crossed paths in the art world and with mutual friends as well. Once I started to paint canvas people started to ask me" have you ever heard of Shawn Forton? Of course I hadn't but I started to look him up and see who he was. I was amazed of course at the amount of players he had done artwork for but also the quality of his work. I eventually became his friend on facebook and Instagram and we began to admire one another. One thing I can say about him is he actually took some of my work when he delivered a piece to Rapper Fat Trel of MMG. He was delivering a painting to him and I ended up doing two hand painted shirts for him which he gave to him as well. A year or two later when the paint parties began me and him were the two biggest small companies doing them in Harford County. I believe I did my first maybe a week or wo before him. He inboxed me asking me the best places to get canvas, easels and all the necessary supplies to run a paint party. Of course I gave him any information I had with no problem seeing what he did for me with getting my shirts to Fat Trel. On top of Shawn Forton, like I mentioned earlier Aaron Maybin, artists like Ron Bass, Chris Brown and even other locals who blew up on social media like Delano Brown. Delano Brown is a young artist from Baltimore who got money and fame by painting unique roses on clothing and other products for people and quickly started to do them for celebrities. I think he was charging five hundred to one thousand for a pair of custom boots and the customer had to supply the boots. I hear her made 1.5 million in one year by releasing his limited edition t-shirts with his hand painted designs on them. He would paint the shirt live on Instagram and put out a post that people can order duplicates of the shirt for 72 hours. He would get maybe one thousand orders and use the orders to go get the shirts printed. This formula made him over a million in one year. When I met Daymond John for the first time he actually gave me advice to do what Delano did. Of course it sounded like a plan and I did actually try it. It worked on a small scale for me but I didn't have the followers or celebrity clientele at the time to be able to see the same numbers he saw but it was a learning experience to know how he worked his customers. I followed many more on Instagram and even those who are famous like Chris Brown. I have done shows with artists from Washington DC, Philly and New York as well. One of the most recent guys I met is a guy by the name of Demont Pinder. This was another artist like Shawn Forton. I would go places, live paint and vend with my art and in DC people would always ask me " Do you know Demont Pinder?" I had never met him until one day me and my wife were going to Lil Mo's birthday and Love and Hip Hop watch party. Rushing home from work and more I didn't have time to whip Lil Mo a painting up for the party. When I get there after about 30 minutes I see a guy walk in with a blank canvas. It's Demont Pinder! He is there to live paint a picture of Lil Mo on the spot. Of course I regret not painting myself but I was happy to be able to meet him and build with him. We talked and I watched his techniques in amazement as he painted Lil Mo without a sketch or anything.(I sketch my live paintings first) while painting her he is giving me all kinds of advice on making a homemade display wall to cheap flights to Miami for Art Basel which is the biggest art show in US easily every year in Miami. It was great connection and great to get some advice from another well respected artist in the DMV. Most artists see others as a threat to them moving forward but if you are smart you will know that you can learn and sponge information off other artists who are willing to build and share information with you.

BRANDING YOUR ART

In order to be noticed by a large number of people, Branding is key for any business and may be even more important for an artist. How to brand yourself and your art will determine if you standout or blend in. As mentioned in the earlier chapter "what kind of art" a big part of branding is to determine what you will be known for. Along with the type of work you are known for, some other factors that will help branding will be your signature or a trademark stamp on each piece similar to the Basquiat crown or many other stamps used by artists. This stamp or signature will be how the public and everyday people separate your work from the field. I tend to use my signature and the year on the painting but I also have an abstract style background where I quote words, lyrics and random quotes around my subject to cover my negative space. Another way to focus on branding yourself is through all your social media sites and an internet presence. This includes fan pages on Facebook, getting as many people to like it as possible, constantly updating the page and sharing your page regularly. A Like page is important because you can get likes from people outside your friend network which will lead to more customers. This also includes other social sites such as Instagram. Instagram has quickly evolved from just a picture sharing app. You can now upload videos, go live and even create temporary stories similar to SnapChat. In addition to how you upload, creating your own hashtag and using hashtags associated with the content is very important on Instagram and Twitter. The hashtag is formally the pound (#) sign which is now used to post trending news, market events and products from various people all over the globe. You should create your own hashtag! Use it on every picture you post to build your hashtag database up. Along with your own you should also post around the subject of the picture you re posting. If I am posting a painting of Muhammed Ali I would use hashtags associated with boxing such as (#boxer, #boxing, #boxingring, #boxinglegend, #legend, #fighter, #ali, and of course add my own #antoniomooreart with many more like #art #boxingart #muhammadali #aliart and more) People click and search hashtags all day and that is how you get followers you would never have or know based on them searching different hashtags and your picture is under that hashtag on Instagram and Twitter. You can use up to thirty hashtags per picture, I suggest using all thirty with every post or close to it for maximum exposure. Another good branding tool is going Live on Facebook. This allows your friends and followers to see you live in action doing your thing. I normally go live while working on a painting, at an event, delivering a piece and more. Friends can comment, share the video, and you can also see how many times the video has been viewed which is a great way to see how many people have viewed your video. Another great way and probably the best way is to get celebrities and people with millions of followers to shout you out. This has happened to me several times and has greatly increased my brand. The first time was Lil Boosie sharing my picture of us on Instagram. It had over 200 thousand likes and thousands of comments. Over the next few years over twenty artists, comedians and different celebrities shared my art on Instagram and snapchat. When Cardi B first left Love and Hip Hop my promoter I work with did her first show. I did her a painting and she shared it on Instagram the next day. Again, the picture had hundreds of thousands of likes and it added some respect to my name in the art world and with celebrities who never knew of my existence. About a year later Cardi had blown up on the charts and had 3 top ten hits on the billboard. She posted a video being thankful for the songs and all her accomplishments. In the video she was standing in her grandmothers' house with my painting on the wall! The video over three days ended up with over 10 million views! 10 million views with my art on the wall is a major branding tool. Other people who shared me on their Instagram pages include Moneybagg YO, Lil Duval, Cassidy, Freeway, Ray J and more. Creating a website is a major branding tool as well. This shows customers you are committed to your brand, are more than local and creates and online store for more traffic along with all social media sites. If you are not working with a lot of capital there are plenty of free sites available, I suggest you buy a custom domain name and link to your site so you are consistently pushing your brand. My website and hashtag are exactly the same so there is no confusion in branding to my customers. Push you brand to the max, it will increase your customer base and eventually increase your revenue.

KNOWING YOUR WORTH

The million dollar question from most artists when they first start out is ' how do I charge" or "how much should I charge." I tell everyone the same thing, make a rate you are comfortable with to start out. When I started painting shirts my rate was thirty dollars an hour. I figured if I make a shirt in thirty minutes minus the costs, thirty to fourty dollars wasn't bad for a twenty year old working for myself. I kept that rate for a few years and at times I made more. I knew the work was worth more but I was new to the business and didn't want to scare people away. I was painting portraits on shirts, cartoons and more which were going for one hundred dollars and more at the mall, I was giving them out for thirty to fifty dollars. As time went on, my work got better, I got a lot more customers and I felt the need to increase my rate and worth yearly. When determining how much to charge for a drawing, painting or any piece of art my advice is to make a rate you are comfortable with and also check out a few competitors who do similar work. As time increased, my business increased and my work got better I felt the need to make more and be worth more. Currently my rate is $250 an hour in most cases I can make more. So, its up to you to know what you are comfortable making and what you can live on after expenses to get the artwork done. How can your work be worth thousand, maybe millions? Very few in the artworld have made millions alive but I feel that will be a thing of the past with social media and the internet. Picasso couldn't sell a panting to someone in another country, Basquiat didn't have Facebook, so imagine if they did? They may have made more while they were alive and paintings may sell for double what they are now. The best way to make your art worth more is to make it limited! Make one or two originals and limited numbered signed prints. When people feel they are buying something "everyone" doesn't own they are more likely to pay for something more exclusive. This is a gray way to increase your worth similar to Delano Brown with his limited edition shirts and how he made money off his Instagram followers. Get your work in the hands of Celebrities. The perception of the everyday person is that celebrities are rich and they all spend a lot of money on stuff. I have donated about 20 pieces to celebrities in exchange for a picture. The fact that billionaires like Mark Cuban own my art makes my art more valuable. Getting your work and footage of successful people with your work is a sure way to increase your worth. Make your work limited, set a rate, increase your rate and your pace and do not be afraid to charge what you are worth.

LEAVING A LEGACY

One thing all artists and people in general want to do is leave a legacy. In art this means to have artwork in certain places, get your legal paperwork done on all art pieces and all the things that can be a legacy after you are no longer here but your art is. Copyrights on every picture, your signature and any exclusive designs are key. This ensures you own your work, the title and everything having to do with that image or piece of work. This also allows you to be able to market your art in a more professional way such as licensing and more. Once copyrights are done, that's when knowing your worth comes into play. Limited edition prints, hosting the piece in art galleries, having piece displayed in hospitals and many places it can be viewed along with making limited duplicates. This ensures your legacy will last forever with your work copywritten and legally registered with the US Copyright office. Another way to leave your legacy is through videos, instructions and even a Youtube channel. This is a great way to leave video of your instructions, pieces of art, events and more that will live on forever and leave your legacy. Set your company up so it can operate long after you are gone. Leave instructions on how day to day operations work, how you think, what partnerships were created and more. LEAVE YOUR LEGACY AT ALL COSTS!

www.ingramcontent.com/pod-product-compliance
Lightning Source LLC
Chambersburg PA
CBHW040312220526
45473CB00002B/641